CW00422329

188 THINGS
YOU SHOULD KNOW ABOUT
MARCELO BIELSA

By Gordon Law

Printed in Europe and the USA
ISBN: 9798699892563
Imprint: Independently published

Photos courtesy of: Maxisport/Shutterstock.com

Also available to buy

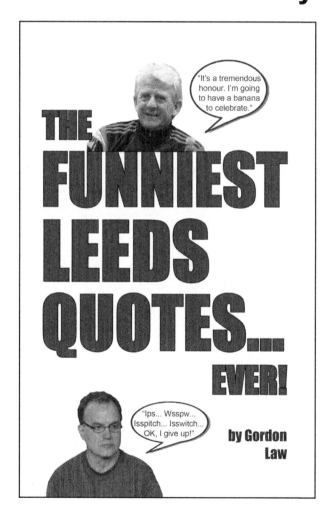

Introduction

Marcelo Bielsa awakened a sleeping giant by taking Leeds United back to the promised land of the Premier League.

Bielsa won his place in the supporters' hearts by not only masterminding promotion but doing so with a thrilling brand of high press and attacking football.

The Argentinian became a meticulous, obsessive student of the game after he quit playing in his mid-20s to become a coach.

Working his way up from youth team boss to manager, Bielsa led Newell's Old Boys to league titles in 1991 and 1992. Stints at Mexican sides Atlas and Club America followed, before he returned to Argentina and won a league crown with Velez Sarsfield in 1998.

A spell at Espanyol in Spain was cut short after he was offered the Argentina national job and he guided the team to Olympic gold in 2004.

Bielsa moved on to become Chile's manager in 2007, before going back to club football with Athletic Bilbao four years later.

After brief spells with Marseille, Lazio and Lille, Bielsa took over at Leeds in 2018. The Whites recovered from losing in the play-offs in his first season to lift the Championship trophy in 2020.

Managing in England's elite division is the latest highlight of Bielsa's illustrious career, which began in 1980 in Rosario, Argentina. Packed with loads of fascinating facts, stats and quotes, this book gives you all you need to know about 'El Loco's' incredible journey so far.

As a player, Marcel Bielsa operated as a defender and liked to burst into midfield or attack if required to win the game.

****

Bielsa says paying a visit to the Great Yorkshire Show in Harrogate helped him settle in the Leeds area. "I visited a fair that gathered many expressions of Yorkshire," he said. "In Argentina I live in the countryside and there are many similarities in Yorkshire to the region I'm from."

Marcelo Bielsa

Known for his immense attention to detail, Bielsa has checked surfaces at the Leeds training ground for dust. After inquiring why there was a boot print on a wall, he was told it was perhaps someone leaning against it. "That shows the person is not concentrated on their work! Unacceptable!" Bielsa exclaimed.

****

Bielsa won the 1991/92 Clausura Tournament of the Argentine Primera Division with Newell's. That season, River Plate had won the Apertura but the league opted against a final decider.

When Bielsa got the Argentina job in 1998, he locked himself in a ranch house in the Pampas area where he watched football from 10am to 10pm. He would break down each game into five-minute segments, noting with coloured pens which team has control of the ball, the scoring chances, the percentage of possession etc and mark points out of 10.

****

Bielsa remained in Mexico after stepping down from the manager's role with Atlas in 1993 to perfect his golf, which he preferred to play alone.

Marcelo Bielsa

A laser-focused Bielsa told his Newell's players before their 1990 Apertura Tournament title decider: "My wife is pregnant and there are complications. I have told her that in an emergency she can call her parents or sister but not me. If one of you needs a telephone for a situation more urgent than that, then you can use it."

****

A graffiti mural of Bielsa in the style of Rio's famous Christ the Redeemer has been created in Leeds in tribute to the manager.

Bielsa is adored by Chile supporters for recording historic wins against Argentina, Paraguay and Peru.

****

At Marseille, Bielsa watched games from an upturned drinks cool box and at Leeds it is an upside down blue bucket. Journalist Guillem Balague explained: "It is his way of dealing with constant back pain that has not left him since his time as a player." Leeds even stocked blue buckets in the club shop for fans to buy for Christmas.

Marcelo Bielsa

Marcelo Alberto Bielsa Caldera was born on July 21, 1955, in Rosario, Argentina.

****

In July 2016, Bielsa resigned just two days after being appointed manager of Lazio. He claimed the Serie A club had not signed the players he had wanted by an agreed deadline. He said: "It was agreed that we would purchase at least four players before July 5. By this date no signings had materialised. Despite that, the club made the contract public despite the fact it was not enforceable without those promises being kept."

When Bielsa led Argentina to Olympic Games' gold in 2004, they became the first Latin American team to win the title in football since 1928 and the first Argentinian Olympic gold medal winners in 52 years.

****

Bielsa owes much of his success in football to his mentor Jorge Griffa who worked with him while an up-and-coming coach at Newell's Old Boys. "Griffa taught me how to understand football. He was a visionary and there wasn't an aspect of the game he didn't master," Bielsa said of the former Atletico Madrid star.

Marcelo Bielsa

Don't ask Bielsa to pronounce Ipswich as he struggled to get the word out when asked about the opponents. "Ips... Wsspw... Isspitch... Isswitch... OK, I give up!" said the Spanish speaker during a Leeds press conference.

****

Bielsa became the first Leeds manager to win the club's opening four games of a season following their 2-0 victory over Rotherham in 2018 – outdoing 35 men who held the job before him.

On joining Leeds in June 2018, Bielsa became the highest-paid manager in the club's history with a reported salary of more than £2million.

****

Bielsa used to take his clothes off and lie on the dressing-room table after losing games as Chile manager. "We walked in and he was completely naked, laying on top of a treatment table like someone was going to perform surgery on him. He was there for about 30 minutes, totally naked," said Mark Gonzalez.

Marcelo Bielsa

Bielsa would instruct players to study the sports pages of newspapers, write up dossiers and even present observations on tactics and set-pieces. It probably contributed to the likes of Gerardo Martino, Eduardo Berizzo and Mauricio Pochettino becoming managers.

****

Bielsa was devastated after his Argentina side crashed out of the 2002 World Cup. A win over Nigeria, defeat to England and draw with Sweden meant a group-stage exit. "It was the saddest thing seeing Bielsa crying," said Juan Sebastian Veron.

In 2003, while Marcelo was managing Argentina, his brother Rafael was Argentina's foreign secretary and his sister Maria (a prominent architect) deputy governor of the Santa Fe province.

****

The well-educated Bielsa often used a thesaurus to simplify his Spanish so his Newell's players could understand his team talks. He would even draw on a player's boots with chalk to indicate where he wanted the ball to be played.

Marcelo Bielsa

There is a network of around 80 football 'disciples' around the world who update the Leeds manager on players, teams and tactics. The ones who impress have an opportunity to become part of his support staff.

****

While Velez Sarsfield manager, Bielsa was invited to the wedding of his striker Martin Posse and turned up that night with a video of his performance against Boca Juniors earlier that day.

Pep Guardiola travelled to Argentina to seek the advice of a number of football personalities before deciding to coach Barcelona B. Bielsa and Spanish film director David Trueba persuaded the retired star to go for it during a barbecue at Bielsa's Rosario ranch where they sat and talked about football for 11 hours.

****

Bielsa lived in the Chile national team's technical centre for three years where he immersed himself studying various coaching methods and tactics.

Marcelo Bielsa

In 1982, Bielsa's first job in football came at the University of Buenos Aires where he coached its team in Argentina's capital.

****

Bielsa admits his reactions to losing are sometimes extreme and difficult to fathom. "For three months our daughter was held between life and death," he said. "Now she is fine. Does it make any sense that I want the earth to swallow me over the result of a football match?"

One of Bielsa's coaches, Diego Flores, replaced Salim Lamrani as the man to translate his instructions to the Leeds players – and he is also by his side to relay his words to journalists.

****

Bielsa added another gong to his collection, by winning the 2020 League Managers Association Manager of the Year award, voted by the LMA membership, after steering Leeds to the EFL Championship title.

Marcelo Bielsa

Bielsa has an impressive record as Argentina national boss, winning 54 and losing 11 out of 83 games, with a 65 per cent win rate. His side scored almost two goals in every game.

****

He took Chile to the 2010 World Cup for only the second time since 1992, which was his second appearance at the global contest. They reached the round of 16, where they were eliminated by Brazil.

Bielsa showed his generous side, helping out a Newell's Old Boys teammate by offering to pay for the roof of a house he couldn't afford. He supported another friend who couldn't have children by paying for artificial insemination and becoming his daughter's godfather.

****

David Beckham's winning goal for England against Bielsa's Argentina contributed to La Albiceleste's exit from the group stage of the 2002 World Cup.

Marcelo Bielsa

An exhausted Bielsa admitted he lost the enthusiasm for the Argentina job and resigned at the end of 2004. He said: "I feel that I no longer have the energy to take on the tasks demanded by la seleccion. I didn't feel I had that drive any more."

****

He successfully sued Club America for compensation for his wrongful sacking in 1996 and took up his old position as sporting director with fellow Mexican side Atlas.

It was heartache for Bielsa after Newell's lost the final of the 1992 Copa Libertadores – the South American Champions League – on penalties to Brazilian club Sao Paulo, featuring Cafu, Rai and Leonardo, after the two-legged affair ended 1-1.

****

Having replaced the sacked first-team manager of Atlas in 1993, Bielsa resigned during the 1994/95 campaign after a series of bad results.

Marcelo Bielsa

It was around the age of 24 that Bielsa began studying coaching manuals while playing for Instituto de Cordoba. "He was already sketching out his career as a coach," said teammate Jose Luis Danguise. "You would go to his apartment and on a piece of paper he would demonstrate how Instiuto should play."

****

Bielsa is so obsessed with dissecting old games of his opponents that he once brought 2,000 DVDs amongst the Argentina team luggage at the 2002 World Cup.

Leeds singer-songwriter and former Britain's Got Talent contestant Micky P Kerr honoured Bielsa with his song Bucket Man, based on the Elton John classic Rocket Man.

****

Former Manchester City boss Manuel Pellegrini has hailed Bielsa's impact as Chile manager. "Bielsa was the one who had more influence on Chilean football because he dared to do more," he said.

Marcelo Bielsa

As Marseille boss, Bielsa had a TV screen and whiteboard installed to the back of a golf buggy, so he could drive it onto pitches at the training ground and instantly explain a tactical change to a player.

****

Newell's Old Boys won the 1990/91 champion-ship decider by beating Clausura Tournament winners Boca Juniors 3-1 on penalties after the two-legged tie ended 1-1. Bielsa was sent to the stands after being incensed at a rash tackle on one of his players.

Leeds asked Bielsa how well he knew the Championship during their interview with him. Bielsa knew every formation each side had used in the division and even calculated the probability for one team's formation to beat another.

****

After his success as manager of Argentina, Bielsa was named the 2001 International Federation of Football History & Statistics (IFFHS) World's Best National Coach.

Marcelo Bielsa

The Catholic Bielsa made a trip to the St Clare
Convent in Guernica with his wife in 2001. He
draped a sign with the words "Poor Clares"
from the bench at a subsequent Athletic
Bilbao match before one of the officials had it
removed.

****

It was Leeds' director of football Victor Orta
who suggested to Andrea Radrizzani that
he should hire Marcelo Bielsa. He knew the
Argentina manager while covering the 2004
Olympics as a journalist.

Bielsa reportedly landed the Leeds job ahead of Antonio Conte, Roberto Martinez and Claudio Ranieri, who were also in the running.

****

Bielsa and Jorge Griffa wanted to see if Mauricio Pochettino had 'footballer's legs' before signing him as a 13-year-old for Newell's. They arrived at the Pochettino home at around 2am and found Pochettino in bed. "They saw me sleeping and Griffa asked: 'May I see his legs?' recalled Pochettino. "My mother pulled the covers off me and they both said: 'He looks like a footballer. Look at those legs'."

Marcelo Bielsa

It has been common practice for Bielsa to employ people to spy on opponents. When he was manager of Chile, he instructed a teenage friend of his daughter to snoop on their opponents in training. The kid was once seen up a tree watching Ecuador's sessions. As Argentina boss, Bielsa used journalist Gabriel Wainer to find intel on the opposition.

****

The manager led Athletic Bilbao to the 2012 Copa del Rey final, but Bielsa's countryman Lionel Messi scored the third goal in a 3-0 defeat to Barcelona.

Bielsa prides himself on being a man of honour. He once gave his Newell's players permission to go to a wedding on the condition they got home by 1am as they had to prepare for a cup game. The players stayed out till 5am, and when the club rejected Bielsa's request to fine them, he resigned.

****

As Chile manager, Bielsa refused to take calls from journalists and the media was kept away from watching his training sessions.

Marcelo Bielsa

The manager endured a frustrating second and final season with Athletic Bilbao. Star midfielder Javi Martinez was sold to Bayern Munich and contract rebel Fernando Llorente was frozen out of the club. Los Leones ended up 12th in 2012/13 and Bielsa was sacked that summer.

****

Bielsa met his wife Laura through his sister – a fellow architect. They have two daughters, Ines and Mercedes.

Bielsa upset Athletic Bilbao club officials by speaking out against the shoddy and late construction of their new training ground which he was overseeing. He apologised after he admitted pushing the site manager out of his office. "The problem is not that the work isn't finished, it was that it was done so badly," he said.

****

Marcelo is the middle child of three siblings with an older brother Rafael and younger sister Maria.

Marcelo Bielsa

Bielsa described his sacking at Lille as the lowest point of his managerial career when he was ousted after just 13 games. "My self-esteem really suffered," he explained. "I was removed from my position with the team in 19th place, though we had only played 20 per cent of the matches for which I was contracted."

****

When becoming Espanyol boss in Spain in 1998, Bielsa was reunited with his old player Mauricio Pochettino, who had joined from Newell's four years earlier.

One of Bielsa's techniques to unwind is by going for a run at night, as late as 2am, listening to his favourite coaching mixtape. While running through the grounds of Argentina's Ezeiza training ground in 1999, he couldn't hear police shouting at him. After finally seeing a dozen guns aimed his way, he hid behind a tree, pleading: "Don't shoot! I'm Bielsa!"

****

A Leeds street has been named Marcelo Bielsa Way in honour of the manager who has helped steer Leeds to the Premier League.

Marcelo Bielsa

When Bielsa instructed his Leeds players to let Aston Villa equalise after a controversial goal, it wasn't the first time he upheld the values of fair play. At a hockey international in 2002, he persuaded the judge to overturn a disallowed goal which would give Germany a win over Argentina.

****

Bielsa's Argentina won the 2004 Olympic Games' gold medal after Carlos Tevez notched the only goal of the match in a victory over Paraguay.

Bielsa is regularly seen walking the two miles from his flat in Wetherby to the Leeds United training ground dressed in full club gear and carrying a backpack.

****

In 1989, Bielsa was elevated from Newell's youth team manager to reserve team boss. "You'd come in for training and there would be so many arrows on the whiteboard that you could barely make out where one ended and another began. You thought the Indians were coming!" said midfielder Gerardo Martino.

Marcelo Bielsa

The rivals of Bielsa's former club, Newell's Old Boys, are Rosario Central. They were formed in 1889 by a group of British workers from the Central Argentine Railway and their blue and yellow kit was based on Leeds United's pre-1961 colours.

****

While at Velez Sarsfield, Bielsa would watch videos of games on a mattress in the back of a van while a staff member drove him home to Rosario.

Bielsa won the 2004 CONMEBOL pre-Olympic Tournament with Argentina, which earned his country qualification for the Olympics that year. They finished first out of 10 teams after winning five and drawing two of their seven matches.

****

Although Bielsa enjoyed success at club level, his appointment as Argentina manager was not universally popular as he had not played for the national side or managed one of the big guns Boca Juniors and River Plate.

Marcelo Bielsa

The Sacred Heart school was where Bielsa was educated and it's one of the most prestigious in his hometown of Rosario.

****

After Newell's lost 6-0 to Santa Fe, the manager locked himself into a room afterwards to reflect on the game. Bielsa said: "I turned off the light, closed the curtains, and I realised the true meaning of an expression we sometimes use lightly: 'I want to die'. I burst into tears. I could not understand what was happening around me. I suffered as a professional and I suffered as a fan."

As manager of Chile, Bielsa made a notable impact on its players, which included star forward Alexis Sanchez, who said of Bielsa: "I learned a lot from him and it is because of him that I am who I am."

****

Bielsa contributed $2.5million of his own money towards the cost of building a hotel at Newell's training ground, which opened in 2018. Named Hotel Jorge Griffa after his mentor, Bielsa wanted to give something back to his home club that was integral to his success.

Marcelo Bielsa

Bielsa played as a defender for Newell's Old Boys, Instituto de Cordoba and Argentino, before he retired at 25 after just five years in the game in order to focus on coaching.

****

In training, Bielsa stages a high-intensity 11 v 11 game – with no set-pieces and the ball does not go out of play – known as 'Murderball'. Leeds midfielder Adam Forshaw said: "You replicate a game with high-intensity moments and it gets you really ready for the game on Saturday."

Bielsa was the highest-earning manager in the
Championship at Leeds with a reported annual
salary of 3million euros – only Rafa Benitez
at Newcastle had ever been paid more in
England's second tier.

****

Bielsa's hometown of Rosario is known as a
"semillero" (seedbed) because it has produced
a number of talented footballers such as
Angel Di Maria, Maxi Rodriguez, Mauro Icardi,
Ezequiel Garay and Lionel Messi.

Marcelo Bielsa

He was a fan, player and manager of his local side Newell's Old Boys. The club was formed in 1903 by Claudio Newell, who named it after his English father Isaac Newell who had relocated to Argentina from Kent.

****

Bielsa's former translator, Fabrice Olszewski, once told him: "You are like van Gogh: a genius. But in terms of human relations, it is a bit complicated!" Bielsa once offered to fight Olszewski because he refused to translate his critical comments to a player at Marseille.

While manager of Lille, Bielsa ordered 20
bungalows to be constructed at the club's
training ground so players could sleep beside
the practice pitches.

****

Newell's headhunted Bielsa from his university
coaching role to become their youth team
manager. Former Spurs boss Mauricio
Pochettino was among a number of talented
youngsters he unearthed during a nationwide
hunt for stars.

Marcelo Bielsa

Bielsa was nicknamed El Cabezon, or Big Head, as a youngster.

****

Bielsa reportedly had to be restrained from flying at Jose Luis Calderon at the airport after the Argentina striker criticised his manager to journalists for not using him at the Copa America. Calderon told Bielsa: "It is what I said it was. I was just a decoration. Admit it. Why the f*ck did you bring me?" Bielsa raged: "You're talking rubbish!" Calderon yelled back: "And you're the son of a b*tch."

After Leeds were fined £200,000 over the Derby County spying affair, Bielsa insisted on paying the money out of his own pocket.

****

One of Bielsa's most memorable team talks came ahead of an Argentina World Cup qualifier in Colombia. "There are two types of street fighters," said the manager. "Those who see blood, get scared and immediately go home. And those who see blood, then go in for the kill. Well, lads, I'm telling you, it smells of blood in here." Argentina triumphed 3-1.

Marcelo Bielsa

Bielsa scooped the 2009 South American Coach of the Year as manager of Chile. The award is presented to the best coach of a club or national team on the continent, regardless of nationality.

****

Bielsa ordered one of his assistants to paint a blue line along the route from his Wetherby home to Leeds' Thorp Arch training ground. The idea was for Bielsa to cycle the journey without worrying about getting lost, which would free his mind for the day ahead.

In April 1995, Bielsa took over from fired boss Leo Beenhakker at Mexican giants Club America – but only after he had studied each of their matches on tape from the previous two years.

****

Bielsa's grandfather Rafael was a lawyer who served on the Argentine Supreme Court, was a Professor of Law at the University of Buenos Aires and an honorary professor at The Sorbonne in Paris.

Marcelo Bielsa

Newell's 19-year-old Fernando Gamboa was asked by Bielsa if he would cut off one of his fingers if it meant victory over rivals Rosario Central was assured. The puzzled defender said if he did that, then he would soon lose a whole hand after five wins. The next day, Gamboa scored the opener in Newell's 4-3 win against Rosario.

****

Bielsa suffered the first sacking of his career in 1996 after three straight defeats at Mexican side Club America.

He holds meetings and studies tactics at his local Costa coffee shop in Wetherby and has been seen shopping at Morrisons in his full Leeds training kit.

****

As youth team coach of Newell's, Bielsa divided Argentina up into blocks of 50 square miles and drove his Fiat 167 around the country to set up football tournaments in each one. He and his assistant scouted 1,050 players and travelled almost 3,500 miles, with the best players invited for a trial.

Marcelo Bielsa

Bielsa became a YouTube sensation in October 2014 after he sat on a scalding cup of coffee left for him on a drinks cooler in the technical area at a Marseille game.

****

The Leeds boss sent fitness coach Benoit Delaval to accept the FIFA Fair Play Award in 2019, in Milan, Italy. He said Delaval had "significantly influenced" his decision to allow Aston Villa to score a goal unopposed after Mateusz Klich had netted for Leeds when Jonathan Kodjia was down injured.

After standing down from his post as Argentina manager in 2004, an exhausted Bielsa shut himself away in a convent. "I took all the books I wanted to read," he said. "I didn't take my phone and had no TV. I lasted three months there, after which I started having full conversations with myself. I was going mad."

****

Bielsa has picked up three Championship Manager of the Month awards as Leeds boss – in August 2018, November 2019 and July 2020.

Marcelo Bielsa

When Bielsa arrived at Leeds, he made his players pick up litter at the training ground for three hours. He had calculated that it took the average Leeds supporter that time to earn the money to watch them in action and he wanted the players to appreciate that.

****

When he is not studying football matches, Bielsa watches South American movies. He even sent the Peruvian film director, Francisco Lombardi, a detailed critique of every one of his films.

The media likes to refer to 'Bielsa Burnout' when his incredible physical demands on his players often result in a roaring first half of a season before a major drop-off, as was the case at Newell's, Athletic Bilbao and Marseille.

****

As Chile manager, Bielsa travelled around the country giving lectures in order to raise funds for the cash-strapped Chile FA's training centre. He gave more than 100 talks and the money helped pay for television monitors and pitch improvements.

Marcelo Bielsa

After Newell's lost 6-0 to San Lorenzo in
the Copa Libertadores, a hooligan group
surrounded Bielsa's house and demanded he
come out. The manager appeared at the front
door holding a hand grenade and threatened to
pull the pin if they did not leave. And they did.

****

Bielsa's coaching philosophy is thought to be
somewhere between Argentinian football's
menottista (romantic idealist) and bilardista
(territorial and tactically driven), taken from the
country's World Cup winning managers Cesar
Luis Menotti and Carlos Bilardo.

Bielsa's former club Athletic Bilbao is unique in that since 1912, it only selects players that were born in the Basque region of Spain. It has been praised for promoting home-grown talent, though the rule does not apply to coaching staff.

****

When Leeds won promotion, Marseille boss Andre Villas-Boas posted a photo of him and Bielsa with the caption in Spanish: 'enhorabuena profe' – translated as 'congratulations teacher'.

Marcelo Bielsa

Leeds is Bielsa's 10th club he has managed, having previously been in charge of: Newell's Old Boys, Atlas, Club America, Velez Sarsfield, Espanyol, Athletic Bilbao, Marseille, Lazio and Lille.

****

Newell's honoured Bielsa's success by renaming their El Coloso del Parque stadium to the Estadio Marcelo Bielsa in 2009. Club secretary Pablo Morosano said: "This is a gesture towards a person who did a lot for the club and today carries its name with pride around the world."

After being promoted to first team manager of Newell's, Bielsa won the 1991 Argentine Primera Division in his debut season.

****

Bielsa is affectionately nicknamed 'El Loco' – the crazy one – for all his eccentric exploits. Former Newell's midfielder Gerardo Martino said: "He is called El Loco because the thinkers in football are usually called El Loco." Bilbao's Iker Muniain was asked if Bielsa really is as mad as people say. "No," he said. "He's madder."

Marcelo Bielsa

On joining Leeds, Spanish-speaking Bielsa was not concerned about a language barrier stopping him from getting his message across to players. He said: "The biggest fact that gets players playing is emotion. If you struggle in a language, there are ways other than words of getting your point across."

****

Bielsa launched a legal claim in 2019 against former club Lille for £17million over the profit made from players he signed. He was sacked in December 2017 after just seven months with the French outfit.

Just two months into his role at La Liga side Espanyol, Bielsa was offered the Argentina job to replace Daniel Passarella and he was appointed in September 1998.

****

Bielsa doesn't give one-on-one interviews ever since he was instructed by officials from Club America to only speak to their own outlets. "Why am I going to give an interview to a powerful guy, if that's going to deny someone from the provinces?" he said. The manager prefers to answer questions from journalists in detail at press conferences.

Marcelo Bielsa

A young Gabriel Batistuta was ordered by Bielsa to stop eating alfajores – sweet biscuits covered in chocolate – to get in shape for the team. "When I arrived at Newell's, I was fat, it was as simple as that," said the Argentinian great. "He also taught me to train in the rain and I hated him for it."

****

Bielsa resigned from his position as Chile manager in 2011 after stating he could not work with the new President of the Chilean Football Board Sergio Jadue.

Marseille president Vincent Labrune compared appointing Bielsa to "signing Lionel Messi for 12 months" when he joined the French giants in 2014.

****

When Chile won the Copa America in 2015 and 2016, many in the game have credited former manager Bielsa for laying the foundation for this success while he was at the helm between 2007-11.

Marcelo Bielsa

Patrick Bamford spoke about Bielsa's high levels of perfection at Leeds' training ground. "He's very 100 per cent. To the point where, if his staff aren't putting cones out to the exact centimetre, they get an earful," he said. "He wants everything to be perfect, the way it is in his head."

****

Despite getting knocked out of the 2010 World Cup by Brazil, Chile fans formed a 'Bielsa NO se va!' (Bielsa is NOT leaving) movement for him to remain as coach after it was reported he was leaving the role.

Arrigo Sacchi was Bielsa's inspiration, according to Argentina legend Gabriel Batistuta. "He dreamed about being Arrigo Sacchi whom he constantly watched winning European Cups with AC Milan," said the former striker, who began his career at Newell's with Bielsa.

****

Shortly after arriving at Leeds, Bielsa snubbed an expensive hotel to move into a one-bedroom flat above a sweet shop in Wetherby. Typical of the manager, he reportedly negotiated down the rent of his tenancy agreement.

Marcelo Bielsa

Bielsa's worst win ratio is 22.2 per cent with Spanish outfit Espanyol – but he was only in charge for nine games from July to October 1998.

****

Mauricio Pochettino says Bielsa was "like my father, my second father." He added: "My relationship with him started when I was 12 or 13 years old. He's a great coach. I will always love him because he was a very important person in my career."

At Athletic Bilbao, Bielsa would take exactly 13 steps every time he crossed the technical area. When asked by a reporter why he did this after every Villarreal attack, he replied: "What is coincidence, is that when there's such a nice game going on, someone spends time counting my paces."

****

His uncle Pancho Parola introduced Bielsa to support Newell's Old Boys, whose stadium was just a short walk from his house.

Marcelo Bielsa

Bielsa was suspended by Lille in 2017 after going against club orders to fly to Chile and spend some final moments with his friend Luis Bonini who was dying of stomach cancer. Bielsa reportedly turned down a free upgrade from economy to business class after a flight attendant recognised the former Chile manager. He only lasted seven months at the club.

****

Bielsa's best win ratio as a club manager is 57.9 per cent while at Argentinian side Velez Sarsfield between 1997-98.

At Newell's, Bielsa instructed keeper Norberto Scoponi to intentionally put goal-kicks out for a throw-in. The theory was the midfield could press the opposition and quickly win the ball back high up the field.

****

Having not worked often enough to obtain a work permit for the Leeds job, Bielsa had to get approval from the FA as an exceptional talent. Spurs boss and protege Mauricio Pochettino was only too happy to write a letter to support his case.

Marcelo Bielsa

His father Rafael, nicknamed 'El Turko', was a lawyer, while his mother Lidia worked as a school teacher.

****

The boss admits he felt embarrassed at the Bielsa Rhapsody 2018 charity Christmas single that got to No.5 in the iTunes charts. He said: "When you receive affection, it is something you are very thankful for. But we have to be very careful when we see the reasons why we receive this affection. In this case, I don't think I deserve the recognition I'm getting. I feel ill at ease."

The Leeds boss admits he should speak English but claims he doesn't have enough hours in the day to study it. "I can never find the time to learn it a little bit more," he said. "When you work in one country, which is not your own country, you are obliged to speak the language of the country."

****

Bielsa can be seen most nights eating dinner at his local Italian restaurant Sant Angelo, in Wetherby. Along with cuisine from Italy, he said: "I like fish and chips... but I enjoy steak from Argentina even more."

Marcelo Bielsa

Bielsa is set to surpass his record of 112 matches at Athletic Bilbao over the 2020/21 season with Leeds, making it the highest number of games amassed at any one club.

****

Before he became Leeds manager, Bielsa surprised the club delegation by getting hold of blueprints for their new Thorp Arch training ground. He made a number of recommendations, which included a first-team dormitory for siestas and a relaxation room, complete with PlayStation and log burner for players to take turns in maintaining.

Bielsa reads one book each week on psychology and uses methods he learns as part of his management technique, often sharing articles or video clips to the Leeds players on WhatsApp.

****

While on a flight to England to cover matches at Euro 96, the football-obsessed Bielsa said to his friend Jorge Valdano from his Newell's days: "After you have lost a game, do you ever think about killing yourself?"

Marcelo Bielsa

The centre half made his Newell's Old Boys debut, aged 20, in March 1976 in a 2-1 defeat at home to River Plate.

****

Benjamin Mendy, who played for Bielsa at Marseille, spoke about the manager's devotion for the game. He said: "When he talked about strategy, you could see the madness coming out. You could see his passion. You could see that he lived for football, for every detail. After the meeting, a teammate looked at me and said, 'He is not normal, this one'. He was right. Bielsa is not normal. Who wants normal?"

It was at Newell's where Bielsa adopted his version of 'total football' where no player was fixed in one position, with midfielders operating in defence and moving the ball swiftly from defence to attack.

****

When Leeds star Kalvin Phillips was given his first England call-up, Bielsa gifted him one of his most-treasured Newell's shirts to mark his achievement. "It was a very nice touch. I'm going to ask him to sign the shirt and will frame the note [to my family]," said Phillips.

Marcelo Bielsa

Pep Guardiola once described Bielsa as "the best coach on the planet". In 2012, he said: "I wish I had been his player he had trained. I appreciate someone who plays so daring. It doesn't matter who he leads: he always has authentic and attacking teams. He is different from all the technicians in the world."

****

Bielsa has paid tribute to his mother Lidia for shaping the person he is. "She was fundamental in my life. For her, no [amount of] effort was sufficient," he said.

When Bielsa was asked by a group of young Bilbao fans to sign their sticker album, the manager refused and took it off them. He told them to meet him at the same place the following day where he returned the album with the entire team having signed it.

****

Leeds have built a small apartment with bed, shower and kitchenette at the training ground by Bielsa's request so he can be fully immersed in planning for games.

Marcelo Bielsa

Former general manager of Real Madrid, Jorge Valdano, spoke about Bielsa's inquisitive nature. "Bielsa machine-guns you with questions," said the Argentine. "You're at a restaurant and he asks the waiter: 'Do you have pear tart?' 'Yes'. 'And is it good?' 'Very good'. 'Then could you give me a slice, but one big enough to accommodate a whole pear?' And so on. That's the kind of guy he is, but also he is the most fantastic friend to have."

****

After three years out of the game, Bielsa became Chile manager in the summer of 2007.

While Argentina manager, Bielsa asked his players to vote on whether to play with his preferred back three or a four. They picked the latter. "That shows what you lot prefer, but we are playing three at the back. Ciao," said Bielsa.

****

When the coronavirus shutdown ended, Bielsa insisted that Leeds United's long-serving chef Izzy be the first person they brought out of furlough.

Marcelo Bielsa

The manager led Velez Sarsfield to Argentina's Torneo Clausura title in 1998 and he lost just one game in his only season at the club.

****

When Leeds owner Andrea Radrizzani and director of football Victor Orta first met with Bielsa at a Bueno Aires hotel, he had watched 17 Leeds matches and knew the names and characteristics of the entire squad, including reserves.

You will rarely see Bielsa in anything other than a Leeds United tracksuit since he moved to Yorkshire. He even wore club apparel at the club's formal black tie centenary dinner. Afterwards, he wrote to the board to apologise as he said he had packed only tracksuits.

****

Bielsa returned from stints at Mexican outfits Club America and Atlas to become manager of Argentinian side Velez Sarsfield in August 1997.

Marcelo Bielsa

The Eleven Paths to Goal was a book Bielsa wrote while he was managing Chile and Athletic Bilbao. Former Scotland boss Craig Brown described it as one of the finest coaching manuals.

****

Aged 25, Bielsa hung up his boots after ending his playing days with Argentina de Rosario in the third division. "He didn't have the ability to be a great player but he had the idea of what one was," said his mentor Jorge Griffa.

Bielsa has yet another nickname – at Marseille he was known as 'le professeur'. It is probably due to his status as a football intellectual and desire to keep a distance from his players.

****

To help him de-stress or get in shape, Bielsa used to visit a health farm run by Seventh-Day Adventists in the Argentine province of Puiggari. The clinic specialised in detox programmes, vegetarian food and hydrotherapy.

Marcelo Bielsa

Bielsa's influence has had a lasting impact as many of the players from the Newell's XI that won titles in the early-90s have gone into coaching. "From that 1990-92 team, nine have become coaches, another an agent," said former striker Cristian Domizzi. "That tells you a lot. Any one of us will have 95 per cent good things to say about [Bielsa]."

****

Bielsa got his first job in Europe as manager of Barcelona-based club Espanyol in June 1998.

The manager always seeks perfection. If players do not hit his daily weight targets or running stats, they simply don't play.

****

A fluid 3-3-1-3 is Bielsa's favoured formation which he has implemented at many of his clubs. It means a team can play with six midfielders, also operating as full-backs, behind a central striker in a pressing style.

Marcelo Bielsa

Former Marseille assistant Jan Van Winckel spoke about Bielsa's extensive tactical knowledge. "I compare Bielsa to a genius because I have never seen anyone structuring football as he does," he said. "You have 24 systems of play, 16 ways to take a free-kick, 24 different passes from the back..."

****

Bielsa's family are immensely proud of him and brother Rafael finds a way to watch every Leeds game back in Argentina.

While Bielsa was studying coaching manuals, he ran a newspaper kiosk along with his friend where they sourced a number of sports magazines from all over the world, which Bielsa would read from cover to cover.

****

The manager twice made Newell's Old Boys champions of Argentina and they were just a penalty shoot-out away from being crowned champions of South America in 1992.

Marcelo Bielsa

Bielsa had an unorthodox method of observing players while at Newell's, recalls Ricardo Lunari. "One day we turned up for training and Bielsa was nowhere to be seen," he said. "We heard his screams, his instructions, but we couldn't find him. Then suddenly someone spotted him. He was up a tree looking for the best view of our training."

****

Unlike most high-profile managers, Bielsa has no agent and uses his brother Rafael to handle a contract's legal technicalities.

After joining Leeds, Bielsa demanded the hillocks in between two of the training pitches be removed as he felt it could mentally disrupt the players.

****

Following the pain of narrowly losing the 1992 Copa Libertadores final, Bielsa departed to Mexican club Atlas in a sporting director role. "I needed to iron out some exaggerated aspects of my character. It was in Mexico that I became a more reflective person," he said.

Marcelo Bielsa

He steered Ligue 1 pacesetters Marseille to a club record-equalling eighth straight league win in October 2014. "I didn't know Marseille had pulled off such a run of results before," he said. "It gives me great joy that we have managed it."

****

Bielsa oversaw 56 victories during his first 100 games with Leeds, giving him the best winning ratio of any manager in the Whites' history (56 per cent).

Bielsa is unfazed by a packed stadium of fans jeering him – he even enjoys it. As Argentina boss, he got abuse from thousands when he attended a testimonial game at the stadium of Boca Juniors. "It is the essence of football," he said of the fans' response to him.

****

You might not notice how tall the Leeds manager is when he's sat on his bucket in the technical area. But the Argentinian measures up at six feet.

Marcelo Bielsa

The dedicated Bielsa admits he always has tactics and formations on his mind. He once told one of his players: "While you're sleeping, I'm thinking of ways for the team to win."

****

Bielsa's daughter had trials with the Argentina women's hockey team. The manager penned an emotional letter to the association on their 20th anniversary in 2020. Las Leonas won silver at the 2000 Sydney Olympics.

In 1977 his political activist brother Rafael disappeared, so Bielsa asked to cancel his contract with Instituto de Cordoba to return to his home town Rosario. Rafael was suspected to be an opponent of the military junta and was held at an illegal detention centre.

****

After winning his first manager-of-the-month award with Leeds, Bielsa declined a request to be photographed with the prize and gave it to the club's head of communications.

Marcelo Bielsa

Bielsa has been known to argue so furiously with Leeds director of football Victor Orta, that those who hear them wonder if they will ever speak to each other again.

****

Ahead of his first pre-season friendly for Leeds against Forest Green, Bielsa asked for full videos and analysis of three games their opponents had played against non-league sides.

After limited playing time with Newell's Old Boys, Bielsa went on loan to regional league side Instituto de Cordoba. Here, he spent his spare time learning to tango and reading books.

****

Bielsa convinced Leeds to create more car parking spaces at the training ground after complaining that the morning chaos was causing too much stress at the start of the working day.

Marcelo Bielsa

Leeds staff were amazed to find that Bielsa's analysts had produced an eight-page document on the third-choice goalkeeper at a bottom-end Championship club, such is his obsession with preparation.

****

Bielsa shows he cares about Leeds' future stars after he spent 19 hours during the coronavirus lockdown analysing videos of their 20-year-old academy midfielder Alfie McCalmont.

Bielsa was pursued by West Ham in 2015 but harboured doubts about his ability to work with the club's owners.

****

Lazio were not amused when Bielsa quit after just two days in the job because of perceived broken promises. "We note with amazement the resignation of Mr Marcelo Bielsa... in a clear violation of the commitments undertaken in the agreements signed last week," said a club statement.

Marcelo Bielsa

Bielsa guided Athletic Bilbao to the 2012 Europa League final in his first season, beating Paris Saint-Germain, Manchester United and Sporting CP on the way. They lost 3-0 to Spanish rivals Atletico Madrid.

****

Bielsa's Argentina suffered penalty shoot-out heartache in the 2004 Copa America final, losing 4-2 to Brazil on spot-kicks after the match ended all square at 2-2.

Printed in Great Britain
by Amazon